old ways through Wester Ross

compiled by
Christopher J. Uncles

By the same author:

Last Ferry to Skye
Lochaber and the Road to the Isles
Easter Ross and the Black Isle

From time immemorial the ferry-boat had provided a vital link for those travelling the ancient hill-tracks and primitive roads between the parishes of Kintail, Lochalsh and Glenelg.

Stenlake Publishing
1999

First published in the United Kingdom, 1999,
by Stenlake Publishing
Telephone / Fax: 01290 551122

ISBN 1 84033 048 1

ACKNOWLEDGEMENTS

The help given by local people in responding to queries or giving permission to reproduce photographs is gratefully acknowledged, and thanks are due to:

Ian Macleod (Dingwall Museum Trust); Janette French and Donald MacIntyre (Gairloch Heritage Museum); Juliet Rees and Frances Ross (Ullapool Museum); Fred Brown of Altnaharrie; Caroline and Tony Fenwick of Langwell; Elaine Kellett of Charleston; the late Alex J. MacBeath of Kishorn; Audrey Mackie of Carn Dearg and Mrs C. M. Maclean of Achtercairn.

Except where otherwise attributed, all the material is from my own collection. Eric Sutherland generously permitted reproduction of pictures taken by his late grandfather, the well-known Dingwall photographer F. W. Urquhart, an appreciation of whom appears in *Easter Ross and the Black Isle*. Finally, thanks are due in no small measure to my wife, Angela, for her practical help and inexhaustible patience.

Rising steeply from quite low ground to a height of 2,009 feet, the buttress of red Torridonian sandstone, known as An Stac, has been weathered and eroded over several hundred million years into a comb of rock bristling with pinnacles – once described as a 'petrified hedgehog'. Stac Polly is a focal point among several strange-shaped peaks which give such a special character to this part of the Ross-shire/Sutherland border.

INTRODUCTION

Many who have travelled the world claim that there is no finer scenery anywhere than that to be found in this north-west region of Scotland. The immensity of the setting of mountain, glen, loch and seascape can in turn be so exquisitely beautiful or, by a weather change, sinister and intimidating that human pretensions are cut down to size, compelling thoughtful reflection.

Wester Ross has been shaped by the elements – the sun, wind, rain and most importantly, by ice. Great forces of glaciation were once at work moulding a landscape of great complexity and stark grandeur. The mountains lying to the north of Loch Carron – the reddish peaks of Torridonian sandstone, tipped here and there with quartzite (often mistaken for snow), are considered to be among the oldest rocks in the world. This mountainous hinterland is pierced by great sea lochs (Broom, Ewe, Torridon, Carron and Alsh).

It is an odd paradox that the seaboard faces the islands of the Hebrides and the Atlantic Ocean on the same latitude as Labrador, and yet the comparatively warm waters of the North Atlantic Drift, originating in the Gulf of Mexico, enables palm trees to grow in Plockton and tropical plants to flourish in the world famous gardens of Inverewe. At Braemore, too, gardens bloomed where there was once wilderness, and in 1938 on Tanera More, the largest of the Summer Isles, the pioneer ecologist Dr (later Sir) Frank Fraser-Darling transformed a barren island into a productive farm, an achievement which attracted national interest. The rich resources of the Minch fishing grounds caused Ullapool to be developed as an important port in 1788, and were also a factor in the establishment of a rail-head and new port at Kyle of Lochalsh in 1897. Quite incidentally, the bringing of the railway to Kyle created an added attraction – the most scenic of train journeys – hailed as one of 'The Great Railway Journeys of the World'.

There have been other influences too. Norse raiders once settled these western lands leaving reminders of their occupation in so many place names. In the eighteenth and nineteenth centuries the notorious Clearances left vast areas of the Highlands and Islands depopulated as hundreds of thousands of crofters, whose families had occupied the same land for generations, were forced overseas to start a new life. So much sadness, still vividly recalled, amidst so much natural beauty.

Old Ways Through Wester Ross is a collection of photographs which complements my previously published book *Easter Ross and the Black Isle* to give a view of mainland Ross and Cromarty (now part of Highland Region) before the Great War. Administered from Dingwall, Lewis at one time formed part of this county, but unfortunately space does not permit its inclusion here. Much has altered since these photographs were taken. In particular there have been fundamental changes to the infrastructure since 1940, brought about by the volume of traffic now carried on small roads which had themselves developed from ancient hill-tracks. The Glen Loyne road was abandoned to a hydro-electric scheme, and the ferries at Dornie, Kyle of Lochalsh and Strome made redundant by bridges or roads. Today's motorist can now enter Kyle by an approach from Balmacara along the shores of Loch Alsh, drive directly from Shieldaig to Torridon through the Balgy Gap, and tour the North Applecross peninsula past decaying townships by 'the road that came 50 years too late'. All quite unthinkable not so many years ago.

The photographs have been arranged in two sequences; Tomdoun to Shieldaig, and Garve to the Summer Isles. Safe journeying!

Christopher J. Uncles

Ullapool Public School, 1912.

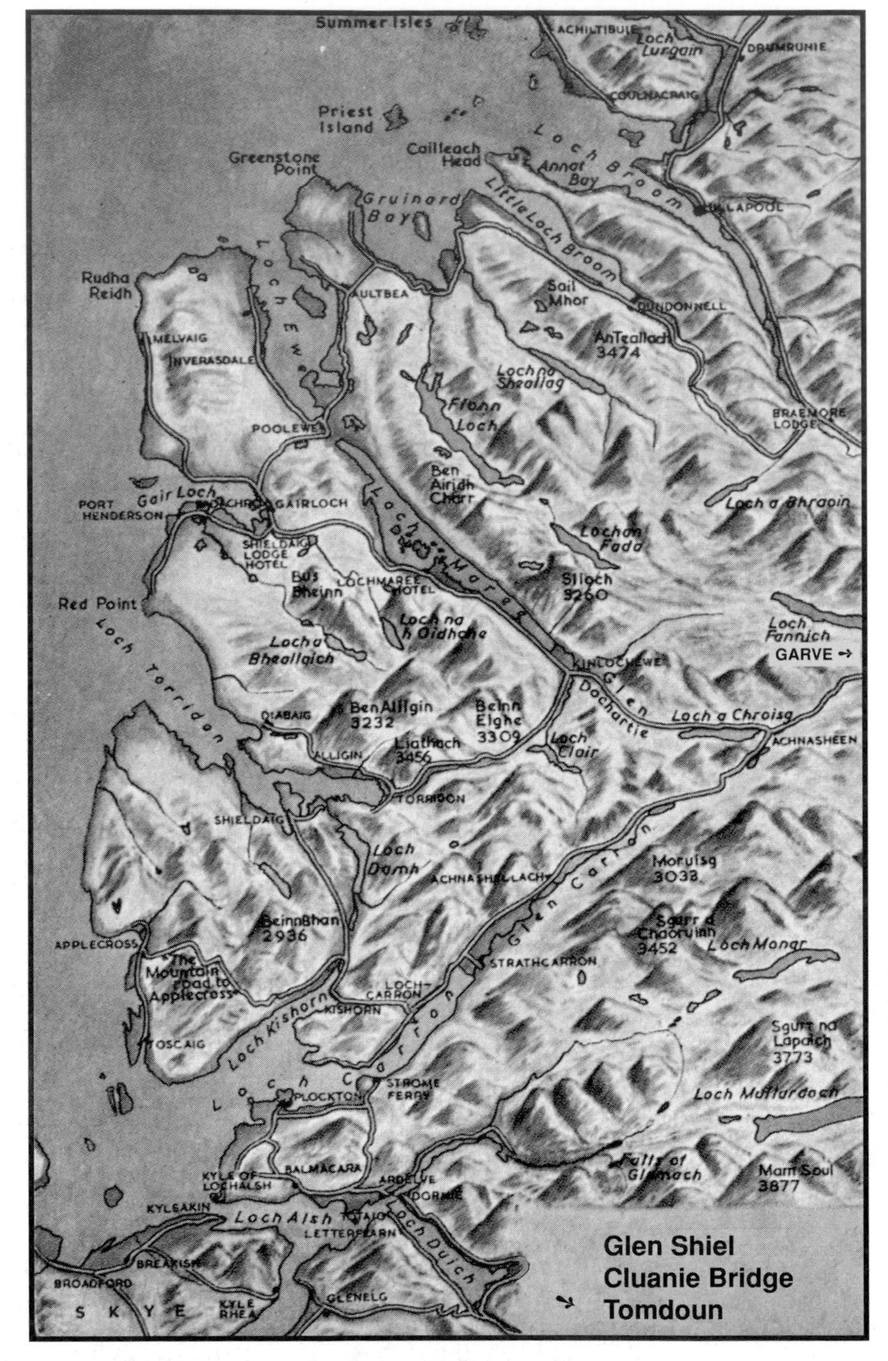
Summer Isles
Achiltibuie
Loch Lurgain
Drumrunie
Coulnacraig
Priest Island
Cailleach Head
Loch Broom
Annat Bay
Greenstone Point
Gruinard Bay
Little Loch Broom
Ullapool
Rudha Reidh
Loch Ewe
Aultbea
Sail Mhor
Dundonnell
Melvaig
Inverasdale
An Teallach 3474
Loch na Sheallag
Fionn Loch
Braemore Lodge
Poolewe
Ben Airidh Charr
Port Henderson
Gair Loch
Gairloch
Loch a Bhraoin
Shieldaig Lodge Hotel
Lochan Fada
Loch Maree
Bus Bheinn
Lochmaree Hotel
Slioch 3260
Red Point
Loch na h Oidhche
Loch Fannich
Loch Torridon
Loch a Bhealaich
Kinlochewe
GARVE →
Glen Dochartie
Diabaig
Ben Alligin 3232
Beinn Eighe 3309
Loch a Chroisg
Liathach 3456
Loch Clair
Achnasheen
Alligin
Torridon
Shieldaig
Loch Damh
Glen Carron
Achnashellach
Moruisg 3033
Beinn Bhan 2936
Sgurr a Chaoruinn 3452
Loch Monar
Applecross
"The Mountain road to Applecross"
Strathcarron
Lochcarron
Kishorn
Loch Kishorn
Sgurr na Lapaich 3773
Toscaig
Loch Carron
Strome Ferry
Plockton
Loch Mullardoch
Falls of Glomach
Balmacara
Kyle of Lochalsh
Ardelve
Dornie
Mam Soul 3877
Kyleakin
Loch Alsh
Letterfearn
Loch Duich
Glen Shiel
Cluanie Bridge
Tomdoun
Breakish
Broadford
SKYE
Kyle Rhea
Glenelg

WESTER ROSS

TOMDOUN TO SHIELDAIG

Tomdoun lies on the northern fringe of Lochaber at a point on the minor road to Kinloch Hourn where the old route from Invergarry to Glen Shiel and Skye struck northwards into Ross-shire. Once cattle were regularly driven this way to the large trysts at Crieff and Falkirk, and this hotel stands on the site of a former inn with which the old-time drovers would have been well acquainted.

Narrow, single track roads, often poorly surfaced, with blind summits, tortuous bends and few passing places – such was the lot of the early motorist, and that, too, on the so-called main roads in remote Highland areas! Perhaps the driver of this Ross and Cromarty registered Morris Bullnose had been paying too much attention to the scenery when he came to grief in this ditch in 1924.

Rising steeply from Tomdoun, the eleven mile stretch of rough mountain road to Cluanie Bridge and Glen Shiel crossed desolate Glen Loyne by two bridges. It also crossed the Inverness-shire/Ross and Cromarty boundary. But, nearly 40 years ago the wild charms of Glen Loyne were sacrificed to a hydro-electric scheme, one of many in this locality, and this road now lies abandoned under the raised water levels of a much enlarged man-made loch.

Prior to the flooding of Glen Loyne, the road rose to a height of 1,424 feet to the top of the pass which afforded stupendous views over a panorama of mountain ridges, lochs and deer forests. Descending by easy gradients around the shoulder of Creag-a-Mhaim, past the lodge (the haunt of stalker and fisherman) to the inn at Cluanie Bridge, the road joins another ancient highway to the west, that from Fort Augustus.

The narrow ribbon hugging the mountainsides is sometimes described on old maps as a 'Wade' road, after the General more often recalled for his road-making abilities than his military exploits, although there is much evidence to refute this attribution. What is beyond dispute, however, is that those renowned travellers and diarists, Dr Samuel Johnson and James Boswell, rode this way in 1773 while undertaking their famous tour.

Better than any number of words, this photograph conveys the sense of wildness and total isolation of the lonely whitewashed inn on this 'road to the isles', set amid towering mountains rising to over 3,600 feet.

Once an old change house and drovers' inn, from time immemorial the Cluanie Inn provided a place of hospitality and welcome for the traveller, and food and shelter for his animal. Today it is a haven for fishermen and stalkers – and an ideal base for 'Munro-baggers'.

At one time, to the frustration of many a motorist, a large body of magnificent Cluanie Highlanders seemed to have a continual 'gathering' on the highway between the inn and the entrance to Glen Shiel.

Faochag (3,010 feet) and The Saddle (3,314 feet), Glen Shiel. Part of the defile is sometimes referred to as the Pass of the Spaniards, commemorating the routing of Jacobite and foreign troops by Hanoverian forces in 1719. Glen Shiel, 'the finest of Scottish glens', is deep and narrow, pierced by roaring torrents, and its tightly-packed, strangely sharp-peaked mountains evoke a Wagnerian atmosphere. One does not easily forget Glen Shiel.

For 10 miles the road unfolds through the glen, past the Shiel Inn (left) to the shores of Loch Duich where routes diverged. Travellers for Kintail and Lochalsh would necessarily cross the river by a second bridge (Shiel Bridge), while those bound for Glenelg and Skye would take the ancient hill track over the heights of Mam Ratagan, visible (left) in this photograph of 1900.

The Shiel Inn, once a popular hostelry, closed in 1907 when sporting considerations took precedence over tourists, and the building was renamed Glenshiel Lodge.

Against a backdrop of the Five Sisters of Kintail and Loch Duich far below, the high road over Mam Ratagan crosses the Inverness-shire boundary making a tortuous climb from sea-level to a height of 1,116 feet, with a maximum gradient of 1 in 5. In September 1773, Boswell and the tetchy Dr Johnson crossed the pass laboriously on horseback, an experience which strained their relationship. They reached the damp and evil-smelling inn at Glenelg at dusk to find food for neither travellers nor their horses. After an uncomfortable night they crossed to Skye.

Picturesque structures of stone and turf or thatch at Letterfearn on the southern shore of Loch Duich belie the realities of life for these dignified people, whose homes lacked any of the basic necessities taken for granted today. It would have been a desperately hard struggle to eke out a living from crofting and fishing, just to maintain a family at subsistence level, during the closing years of Queen Victoria's reign.

In 1846 the failure of the potato crop owing to blight brought deprivation and famine to Kintail and Lochalsh (as elsewhere), leaving many destitute amid scenes more often associated with third world countries today. The fishing depended on the vagaries of the herring catch, and there were often poor years. However, some were spectacular as in 1791, when in July the minister of Kintail reported that 50 boats were overwhelmed by the sheer abundance of herring in Loch Duich.

Large numbers of people welcomed King Edward VII when he came ashore at Letterfearn on 21 September, 1904. Here he is on the jetty constructed specially for the royal visit to Loch Duich, and which has been known since as the Royal Pier.

The 1904 visit was such a success that it was repeated exactly a year later. Here His Majesty is seen at Letterfearn, embarking for Lord Burton's yacht, lying offshore and out of sight in this photograph.

Druidaig Lodge, Loch Duich, as it was in 1906.

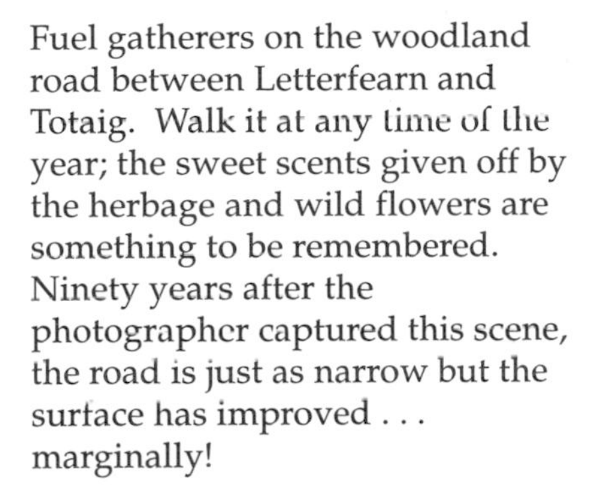

Fuel gatherers on the woodland road between Letterfearn and Totaig. Walk it at any time of the year; the sweet scents given off by the herbage and wild flowers are something to be remembered. Ninety years after the photographer captured this scene, the road is just as narrow but the surface has improved . . . marginally!

The road around this shore of Loch Duich ends at the former ferryman's house and jetty at Totaig (photographed by the author in 1969). Situated at the confluence of three sea lochs, Totaig was of strategic significance having a foot passenger connection with the Dornie/Ardelve ferry a mile away across the loch. Ships once brought all manner of freight to this remote place, together with news from the outside world. In an earlier age before mass communication little slipways such as this were convenient places to exchange news.

The group of peaks known as the Five Sisters of Kintail form a magnificent panorama at the head of Loch Duich, and the impressive view across the loch can cause one to reflect on the insignificance of man in this often overwhelming landscape. Seen here sometime before the Great War, the parked touring car bears an original Wigan registration plate.

The tiny clachan of Carn Gorm had welcome facilities for the motorist, *c*.1920. A causeway now carries the main road to the west across this inlet at the head of Loch Duich, leaving a loop of the former highway around Morvich and Croe Bridge which is ideally suited to walkers.

The church at Clachan Duich has been roofless since 1719. Generations of MacRaes sleep in this ancient burying ground of Kintail, in the shadow of the long ridge of Ben Attow (3,385 feet).

Internal rivalries for the prestigious position of Chief in individual clans are as old as the hills themselves. In this respect, the scene being played out within the crumbling walls of the church on 30 July 1927, is not without interest. The memorial on the ground being unveiled to Sir Colin George MacRae WS (1844-1925) is inscribed as having been placed there by clansmen and clanswomen 'in loving memory of their Chief', despite the fact that in 1909, Lord Lyon King of Arms had refused Sir Colin's petition for official recognition as Chief of the Clan MacRae! In that decision the MacRaes of Conchra won the day, and a memorial close by details *their* lineage. The rival memorials face each other and gather dust; the war of words continues silently, even in death.

Clan MacRae Gathering at Clachan Duich, 30 July 1927.

Inverinate House, 1906. By the age of 34, Sir Alexander Matheson, Bart., MP (1805-1886) had amassed immense wealth from the Far East trading company, Jardine Matheson & Co., whose fortunes had been founded on the tea and opium trades. Together with other substantial acquisitions of land in Ross-shire, he purchased the Balmacara Estate for £120,000 in 1851, and built Inverinate House and Duncraig Castle.

Eilean Donan Castle, 1901. The island, named after a 6th century Irish saint, became a MacKenzie stronghold in the 13th century. Occupied by Jacobite forces in 1719, it was bombarded and destroyed by Hanoverian ships. It remained a ruin until Colonel MacRae Gilstrap undertook a sympathetic restoration between 1912 and 1932 at a reputed cost of £250,000, then a vast sum. At the time, local opinion varied on the wisdom of restoring a total ruin.

Eillandonan Castle, Dornie.

The Totaig ferry-house lies across the loch, while on the island builders' materials and the partially constructed main tower show that rebuilding is underway. The architect, George MacKie Watson of Edinburgh, and a gifted clansman, Farquhar MacRae of Auchtertyre, were responsible for the superb craftsmanship executed by a body of mostly local workmen. Sadly, Mr MacRae died 6 months before the formal reopening took place in July 1932.

The Clan MacRae War Memorial, Eilean Donan Castle, Loch Duich, Ross-shire.
3464.

Built into an external wall is a shrine bearing names of the Clan MacRae world-wide who gave their lives in the Great War of 1914-1918. The mortal remains of many may lie in some distant foreign land, but their spirits are here in the land of their forefathers. A verse from *In Flanders Fields*, the immortal lines of which were penned by Lt. Col. John MacRae, completes the picture.

Geographical factors and the annual migration of the herring contributed to the establishment of a trading and fishing station at Dornie in the early 19th century. Later, schooners of up to 200 tons were built here. In 1890, the village was described as having a single row of houses facing the sea. They were 'decidedly of a better class' than others in the neighbourhood being 'almost all two storied with slated roofs and small but well-cared-for gardens in front'. This is a reference to Francis Street, seen here in a photograph of *c.*1915.

The road system that exists in Kintail and Lochalsh today had been largely established by 1825. The width of Loch Long (about 220 yards at this point) was an obstacle to free passage between the two parishes, and the Aird Ferry, connecting Dornie and Ardelve, became a vital link. This sequence of photographs shows some of the differing loads rowed across the loch in the early days – foot passengers and sheep . . .

. . . a carriage and pair . . .

. . . and a motor car secured on two wooden planks. A sudden gust of wind from the wrong quarter, or currents too strong for the rowers, could quickly take the ferry-boat off course leading to frustrating delays. Journeying in the Highlands, even in the present century, was not without its hazards.

Aird Ferry: blowing the horn for the ferry-boat. In his book *Western Highlands*, Arthur Gardner, writing after the building of the Dornie Bridge, notes that the Totaig ferryman was summoned 'by a battered horn hanging up by the pier which makes a noise like a cow in extreme agony'.

The military importance of Kyle of Lochalsh and Balmacara in two World Wars was a factor in the building of this bridge across the Loch Long narrows in 1940. Until 1946 a toll was charged. In 1991 a replacement bridge was built at a cost of £6.5m and the original structure was demolished.

Staff pose outside the Airdferry Hotel, *c.*1905. Subsequently enlarged and renamed the Loch Duich Hotel, it can be seen in the previous photograph over the loch among trees to the right of the bridge. In times past a fair or market was held twice a year on the stance below the hotel where cattle and a variety of goods were traded.

This memorial was erected by the Highland friends and admirers of Farquhar Matheson MB, JP (1840-1905). According to the inscription 'he was a devoted friend of the Highland people and took a warm and generous interest in the language, music and literature of the Gael'. One of a series of pictures taken by Dingwall photographer F. W. Urquhart at the unveiling ceremony at Kirkton in 1907.

Sheep graze at Reraig, Balmacara, *c.*1900. The introduction of Cheviot and Blackface sheep by the landed proprietors before 1800 led to the creation of extensive sheepwalks. Crofters were cleared to less productive ground on the margins of the seashore from land their families had occupied for centuries. Subdivision of crofts, the spectacular rise and ultimate decimation of the kelp industry during the Napoleonic Wars, years when the fishing or potato crop failed leaving many destitute, and eviction to the Carolinas or Australia – such was the lot of the Lochalsh tenantry in the 19th century.

Dating from about 1800, Balmacara House stands above a storm-beach overlooking Loch Alsh. At the time of this photograph, *c.*1907, the house and estate were in the ownership of absentee landlord Sir Kenneth Matheson, Bart. Later it became the residence of Sir Daniel Mackinnon Hamilton who purchased the western portion of the Lochalsh Estate and carried out many improvements until his death in 1939. On the demise of Lady Hamilton seven years later, the estate passed into the care of The National Trust for Scotland.

Erbusaig lies on the old road to Kyle of Lochalsh from Strome Ferry and Auchtertyre, completed in 1813. Black houses and well-tended crofts overlooked a picturesque bay with a panorama of islands. Between 1893 and 1897, when the railway was extended from Strome Ferry to Kyle, a huge embankment was thrown across Erbusaig Bay obliterating the views, cutting off the settlement from the sea and disrupting the fishing. For the inhabitants who remained, life was never the same again.

The amount of rock blasting required to bring the 10½ mile rail extension from Strome Ferry to Kyle of Lochalsh made it both the most remarkable and most costly length of track in Great Britain, estimated at £20,000 per mile. The composition of the rock – gneiss and quartz – made it the most difficult type to work. The trackbed was laid in cuttings up to 85 feet deep – a suitable culmination to what many claim to be the most scenic of all rail routes, and a lasting tribute to the skill and tenacity of those Victorian engineers.

Kyle of Lochalsh developed with the arrival of the railway in 1897. Buildings of stone, or often of corrugated iron or wood, sprung up wherever the barren, rocky hillsides permitted, or around the road which entered the village from the north. The exciting air of those early days invited comparisons with the Wild West or a gold-rush settlement, and some of the early pioneers prospered. The snowy mountains of Skye lie across the narrows.

Main Street provided access to the ferry pier and the Station Hotel which overlooked Kyleakin on Skye. The line of the railway lay diagonally through the village, past the large locomotive shed (centre), to terminate beyond the cutting (extreme left) at a newly built island station platform, sidings and pierhead. The picture dates from *c*.1900.

Kyle Hotel, *c*.1900. Before 1897 the village consisted of the Kyle Inn and four houses. Later upgraded to hotel status under proprietor Donald Urquhart to rival the new Station Hotel, the inn claimed to have been established in 1701 and had long catered for the needs of travellers crossing to and from Skye.

This photograph, *c*.1902, shows the Commercial Bank dating from 1896 (right), and the Pioneer Stores (extreme left) owned by Alexander Macrae. Known as 'the Pioneer', he had previously been one of the foremost merchants at Strome Ferry but had moved to Kyle with the railway. This was a canny business decision because while Kyle naturally prospered as the new railway terminus, the fortunes of Strome Ferry rapidly declined.

The changing face of Kyle and a sad end to a link with the early days. The burnt out shell of the Pioneer Stores, photographed by the author in 1985.

Looking up Main Street in 1925 to the hills beyond. The General Post Office Building is on the left.

The Highland Railway acquired Kyle House which began a new life as the Station Hotel in 1897. Facilities included 'coffee-, smoking-, and drawing-rooms and a number of comfortably furnished bedrooms'. The convenience of the hotel's position at the Skye ferry slipway ensured it a place on the itineraries of many. From these humble origins grew the much larger Lochalsh Hotel, such a familiar landmark today.

'Over the sea to Skye' in the last decade of Queen Victoria's reign. The strong currents and heavy loads (later to include motor cars which were specially insured for the crossing) tested both the skill and strength of the rowers until the introduction of the motor-boat in 1914. For those wishing to know more of 'the Misty Isle' my book, *Last Ferry to Skye,* provides a comprehensive armchair tour.

Tinkers wandered over large areas, generally travelling the same routes and becoming familiar visitors year after year. They were horse dealers and seasonal workers on the land at harvest-time but, above all, they were whitesmiths (workers in tin), making and repairing tin utensils for everyday use. Captioned 'Tinkers Crossing to Skye', F. W. Urquhart's photograph, *c.*1905, shows a reluctant passenger being coaxed fore and aft into the ferry-boat.

Hundreds upon thousands of cubic yards of solid rock, there since the Creation, had to be cut, blasted and removed so that the railway could be brought to its destination at a new station and pierhead in the shadow of the mountains of Skye.

Kyle of Lochalsh was nearer to the rich fishing grounds of the Minches than either Mallaig or Oban, and the Highland Railway planned to attract this lucrative traffic away from rival rail companies. Additional revenues would be generated by carriage of livestock and, of course, tourists. The elegant station buildings set on a square-headed pier were located just a stone's-throw from the Skye ferry slipway and Station Hotel, whose roof and chimneys can be seen (right) – all of which made an ideal interchange for travellers.

No doubt there was tension and excitement in the air as Highland Railway directors, officials and their guests awaited the arrival of the first train from Inverness on 2 November 1897. (Photograph reproduced here by kind permission of Dingwall Museum Trust.)

The railway terminus, seen here in the early years, with PS *Lovedale* at the pierhead. She operated the Kyle-Stornoway mail service, but was broken up in 1904.

'Skye Bogie' No. 85, built in 1892, heading a mixed train at the station about 1900. David Jones, locomotive superintendent of the Highland Railway, developed this special rolling-stock to counteract the difficulties experienced on the steep gradients and sharp curves of the Skye line. Combined passenger and goods trains ('mixed trains') were ideally suited to Highland working but did not have a continuous brake facility throughout the length of the train, and there were accidents. Mixed blessings!

During the Great War, between May and November 1918, Kyle became a busy transit station for all types of military equipment, especially mines shipped in from the United States. In this photograph of October 1918 a number of wagons stand on a spur of track (top right). This connected with the adjoining US naval base where personnel were engaged in reloading the explosives for transfer by rail to a depot at Dalmore, near Invergordon, prior to assembly and deployment in the North Sea.

Scenes such as these were once common in the Highlands and Islands. Certain features suggest that this was a private photograph to which was added a postcard back. Signed by a C. P. Anstruther MacKay, it was written from Carver's Croft, Plockton in September 1909.

Plockton, the old 'capital' of Lochalsh, lies 6 miles north-east of Kyle on the shores of Loch Carron. Boat-building, fishing and trading developed around its sheltered anchorage, but in the nineteenth century the village suffered greatly from depopulation due to enforced migration. Today's visitors are tourists and artists attempting to capture on sketch-pad or canvas the stunning views of mountain and loch which make Plockton so widely regarded as 'a jewel of Wester Ross'.

Open-air Communion services were a familiar sight right up to the outbreak of the Great War. Worshippers came from near and far, taking up local accommodation to attend a series of services which began on a Thursday and ended the following Monday (the 'Communion Season'). The wooden kiosk served as a pulpit, providing shelter for the preacher in inclement weather while his congregation had to brave the elements.

During his ownership of the Lochalsh Estate between 1851 and 1886, Sir Alexander Matheson, Bart., MP, built Duncraig Castle among wooded crags in an elevated position overlooking Plockton. During the Second World War the castle served as a naval hospital, and in 1946 passed into the hands of Ross-shire County Council on the Hamilton bequest. Subsequently operated for some years as a catering and domestic science college, this use ended in 1988, since when the castle has lain empty.

'Be it ever so humble, there's no place like home' is the wording inscribed on this *c.*1900 photograph captioned 'Highland Cottage, Strome Ferry' – a world away from the laird's opulent surroundings at nearby Duncraig.

Strome Ferry was the farthest point reached by the new Dingwall and Skye Railway in 1870. Nearly 500 guests attended a celebratory banquet in an engine shed there to mark the opening of the new line. At the conclusion it was reported that generous measures of whisky, claret and port had left few sober, and the bagpipers could neither blow, stand up, nor all play the same tune! Twenty-seven years later the railway was extended to Kyle of Lochalsh. By the time of this photograph, *c.*1900, the new extension was in operation, and this briefly important station and busy fish pier were in irreversible decline.

A steep hill brought the poorly surfaced road past the Station Hotel (centre right) to a stone jetty by the shore – an ancient ferrying-place to North Strome which lay half a mile across Loch Carron. A scattering of houses and the decaying pier, which in former years had provided a link with Skye and Stornoway, completes this pre-First World War photograph.

Station Hotel, *c.*1900. This well-known hotel once had a fine reputation and was well used by those travelling across Loch Carron. Before the road along the southern shore of the loch was opened in 1970, a car ferry operated to and from North Strome. Motorists intent on travelling north, and missing the last Saturday ferry, would be detained here until Monday morning.

Station Hotel, c.1885, and . . .

. . . a 1995 photograph by the author from the same general perspective, two years after the building (latterly named Stromeferry Hotel) had suffered a disastrous fire. As I write, the building remains derelict and its future uncertain.

Vehicles arriving at the Strome Ferry jetty from North Strome. In the early years one vehicle at a time was carried. Despite a subsequent increase in the car-carrying capacity of the ferries, in the closing years long queues would form either side of the loch at peak periods causing substantial delays. The new road around Loch Carron spelt the end for the ferry, and the bottlenecks.

Ardnarff, Loch Carron, *c*.1900. The Gaelic name Ard an Arbha translates to 'the promontory of corn'.

About the time Sir Alexander Matheson was enlarging the Strome Ferry inn to cope with the anticipated extra business the railway would bring, he was also completing an hotel adjoining the equally new station at Strathcarron. Built in concrete, an innovative building medium in 1870, the hotel was photographed by F. W. Urquhart, *c*.1905.

Strathcarron station was built to serve the scattered communities around the glen, and in particular Jeantown (Lochcarron village), four miles distant on the northern shore of Loch Carron. Roses bloom around the platform for Dingwall and Inverness in this 1930s photograph.

To appreciate the extensive lateral development of the village, Lochcarron's gleaming white buildings are best observed from the opposite (southern) shore. The central part was built about 1800, and named Jeantown on the coming of age of the daughter of John MacKenzie of Applecross.

Lochcarron, looking west, *c*.1900. The presence of the ubiquitous herring was responsible for the building of the original settlement here. Note in this photograph poles for drying the fishing nets, and the absence of the low wall on the seaward side of the road – a later feature.

Hugh MacKenzie's general stores, known as 'the Emporium', boasted a Hairdressing and Shaving Saloon. He also advertised Fruit, Confections and Aerated Waters. Such businesses were very few and far between, and tended to stock everything from 'a pin to an anchor', although Mr MacKenzie probably sold few of the latter! There were facilities, too, for the motorist (right) – a lifeline in this far-flung corner of Wester Ross.

In 1819 Jeantown tripled in size after completion of the Great Loch Carron Road between Dingwall and the ferry at North Strome. Thought to date from the late 18th century, the Lochcarron Hotel lies on this important east-west route, and serves travellers today just as it did in years past.

North Strome Inn, *c.*1900. The building lay a few yards from the slipway, providing a convenient stop-over for southbound travellers whose journey might be delayed as no ferries operated on the Sabbath.

An early ferry-boat at North Strome had wooden planks for cars, and long-handled oars for the rowers. Strome Ferry, where travellers would join the Lochalsh road for Auchtertyre, Balmacara and Kyle of Lochalsh (for Skye), lies across the water. Those heading east for Kintail and Glen Shiel would take the Aird Ferry.

Scenes such as this at North Strome have passed into history; the waters quietly lap against the old slipway and nothing disturbs the peace now. Motor-boats were in use when this picture was taken, c.1958, and several vehicles could be carried at a time. But at peak periods there could be a similar queue on the opposite shore when delays might be measured in hours. Frustrating for the motorist, but good business for the ferry-man – especially if he was also the inn-keeper!

'On the road to Kishorn'. The journey northwards into the remote, wild mountainous region of Applecross was not lightly undertaken by the traveller of 100 years ago.

Ardarroch, Loch Kishorn and the majestic grandeur of the Applecross mountains, *c.*1909.

Courthill formed part of the estates belonging to the MacKenzies of Applecross from the 1600s until they sold their lands in 1857. The house was enlarged in 1856 and 1883. Quite scandalously, it was deliberately unroofed towards the end of World War II and subsequently acquired by a demolition contractor. The stark ruins of the mansion fix a bleak gaze on the Applecross mountains; this undated photograph shows the property in happier times.

The 'Kishorn Dwarfs' were born to parents of normal stature. In 1846 they were taken to London to dance before Queen Victoria and were cruelly exploited, being put on show at concerts. At that date, Finlay, Mary and John were aged 22, 18 and 20 years respectively, and their heights were 45", 43" and 44". Finlay, the eldest, died in 1912.

Between the shore of Loch Kishorn and Applecross Bay lies the most formidable of Britain's mountain roads, the Bealach nam Bò (Pass of the Cattle). Over its ten mile length, this former drove road reaches a height of nearly 2,100 feet at the watershed and, even in mid-summer, snow is often present on the summit. Only really suitable for those on foot or horseback at the turn of the century, the sharp curves and steep gradients of up to 1 in 3 presented a severe challenge for a laden horse-drawn vehicle, with the result that loads had to be lightened on occasions.

Such was the nature of the pass that it was used for reliability tests when motoring was in its infancy. The road, once narrow with a high grass-covered ridge in the middle and few passing-places, has been well surfaced throughout its length since 1957.

This is not a road for the faint-hearted motorist as, once committed, there is no turning back. Loch Kishorn lies far below, while the dark cliffs of Meall Gorm dominate the middle distance.

In AD 673 St Maelrubha established a church and sanctuary on the shores of Applecross Bay over which he presided for 51 years. One of the great Celtic saints, his reputed burial here makes Applecross second only to Iona in terms of significance for the early Christian church. The sanctuary of Applecross had a 'girth' or circumference of 6 miles, formerly marked by stone crosses. The Saint's Day is 21 April.

Milton jetty, *c.*1905. Bad weather might close the difficult route over the Bealach for long periods, so that virtually everything required to sustain this remote community came by sea. Twice daily (Sundays excepted) in late afternoon and in the dark early hours, this ferry-boat would rendezvous in the bay with the Kyle-Stornoway boat, SS *Sheila*, to bring ashore passengers, mail and all manner of cargo.

The terrace of houses overlooking the shore is known as 'The Street'. The shop and Temperance Hotel, on the left, were managed by Mr and Mrs Sandy MacRae who were prominent members of the local community at the time of this photograph, *c.*1905.

The Laird's House, *c*.1905. 'The Mansion House, which is delightfully situated near the sea is a commodious building, commanding very charming views. It contains double dining and drawing rooms, 15 bedrooms, nurseries, and ample accommodation for servants', (*The Highland Sportsman and Tourist*, 1883). Lord Middleton, an absentee landlord, collected estates in the way that others collect postage stamps. Continuing the policies of his predecessors, he evicted crofters and their cattle to provide a few weeks' deer stalking for the rich over his 85,000 acre estate.

The Factor's House, *c*.1905. In the early 1800s, North Applecross sustained nearly 1,000 breeding cattle. At the 1851 census the number of inhabitants stood at between 700 and 800. Set amidst stunning views to Skye and the Outer Hebrides, the deserted, ruined townships testify to subsequent neglect. Community need has suffered at the hands of private greed. Recently completed community-led buy-outs elsewhere have resulted in promising partnerships in successful land management. If such a policy could have been implemented here a century ago, depopulation might have been stemmed.

A return over the Bealach enables the traveller to join the road through the glen to Shieldaig, a small village on an arm of Loch Torridon.

Norse invaders once occupied these lands, and they called the bay 'Sild-Vik' (Herring Bay). The village, which has an almost Hebridean atmosphere, is spread along the shore between the sea and neatly tended crofts, which form the immediate hinterland. In 1970, The National Trust for Scotland acquired the 32 acre Shieldaig Island, home to native Scots Pine and a heronry.

The purchaser of this postcard of 'The Street' retained it as a memento of a stay on 22 and 23 September 1926. The house indicated by the arrow is detailed as 'Tigh-na-Fhuiran (The House of the Well), Miss J. Macpherson'.

At one time the motoring road ended at Shieldaig, and those intent on proceeding north could do so only by boat as foot passengers to Torridon village, Inveralligin, or Diabaig (of which more later). A track of sorts, suitable for walkers, led eastwards for 8 miles along the southern shore of Upper Loch Torridon where a road could be joined again. In those days, Shieldaig to Torridon village by car necessitated a 60 mile detour via Lochcarron, Achnasheen and Kinlochewe!

Shieldaig Village and Bay from the north, *c*.1907.

These boys and girls were photographed by the shore at Shieldaig on 22 September 1913. During the summer months (from 1 May onwards) it was customary for children to go barefoot. The Great War, in which a whole generation lost their lives, was less than a year away. One can only speculate on the effects that such a war may have had on their parents and families, and wonder how these youngsters fared in later life; a thought-provoking note on which to ponder before continuing the journey northwards.

GARVE TO THE SUMMER ISLES

The scattered rural community that is Garve ('the rough place'), lies just beyond a loch of the same name, ten miles as the crow flies west of Dingwall, the county town and administrative centre of Ross and Cromarty. Set amidst moorland and rugged mountains, Garve stands at the gateway to the Ross-shire Highlands.

Garve station, on the Dingwall to Strome Ferry railway, opened in 1870. Constructed with an unusually wide gap between the 'up' and 'down' tracks, it had been intended to convey East Coast fishing boats by rail from the canal at Dingwall to Loch Carron, and thereby to the fishing grounds of the west. This would have avoided time-consuming sailings around the Pentland Firth, but financial considerations put paid to the scheme.

This postcard was sold through the well-stocked general store of W. & R. Mackenzie. Such businesses were the mainstays of small communities, and a place to exchange news and gossip.

The hotel developed from a building once known as the Inn of Garve, one of Scotland's oldest inns, familiar to the cattle drovers travelling the north-western glens to the periodic Dingwall stock sales. In 1848, William Duncan Mackenzie was the tenant here. He also acted as post runner to Ullapool, initially conveying the mails on horseback, and later by stage-coach. For 118 years until 1966 (when Miss Helen Mackenzie retired), three generations of Mackenzies ran the Garve to Ullapool mail service and this famous and popular fishing hotel, together with its 28 acre farm.

At the hamlet of Gorstan, one mile north-west of Garve, roads divide. The route by which the mails were carried to and from Ullapool, 32 miles distant, curves away through the deer forests of Strath Garve and past the isolated inn at Aultguish. By horse this journey might have taken 2 days, or a week or longer in heavy snow. An Albion motor-bus replaced the stage-coach in 1912.

Built of pink granite trimmed with blue-gray slate and set in a 40,000 acre estate, the lodge (pictured here *c.*1907) stands high above Loch Luichart, a monument to the golden age of Victorian sporting life. After her husband's death in 1864, Lady Louisa Ashburton made her summer home here. At various times Robert Browning, Thomas Carlyle, John Ruskin, Sir Edwin Landseer and other well-known celebrities of the day were entertained, making the house a literary and artistic salon in the wilds of Ross-shire.

F. W. Urquhart photographed this group on the station platform sometime before the Great War. The original station buildings, in the background, were dismantled in 1954 when the waters of Loch Luichart were raised by 25 feet as part of the huge Conon Valley hydro-electric scheme. This necessitated the building of a new station and length of railway track on a higher level, beyond the reach of the enlarged loch.

There is now no trace of the Station Hotel as the building suffered a disastrous fire one February night in 1995 and the dangerous structure, which adjoined the railway platform, was immediately demolished. In 1877 Murdo MacIver was the hotel proprietor; he also operated the Kinlochewe and Gairloch mail service. A man of stern religious principles, his courteous refusal to provide horses to carry Queen Victoria's mail on the Sabbath during her stay at Talladale (Loch Maree) that year is still recalled in the area.

Queen Victoria arrived by special train at Achnasheen at 4.45 p.m. on 12 September, 1877, having travelled by way of Ballater, Inverness and Dingwall. The station was bedecked with bunting, and a crowd from the outlying area had gathered to welcome her. The royal party included her youngest daughter Princess Beatrice, General Ponsonby (secretary), Sir William Jenner (court physician), the Duchess of Roxburghe, the indispensable John Brown and Her Majesty's collie, Noble. Carriages awaited the train for the 20 mile drive to the Loch Maree Hotel, chosen by the Queen for a holiday.

The shooting lodge at Ledgowan was nearing completion when this photograph was taken *c.*1908. It commands extensive views over the inhospitable hills which surround Achnasheen, and is now an hotel. Some years ago the proprietor showed me some magnificent Edwardian plumbing in one of the bathrooms. In response to my query regarding the number of inhabitants living locally his tally came to no more than 30.

Loch Rosque is a sheet of water 3½ miles long, and the lodge at its eastern end was once the home of the late Sir Arthur Bignold MP, a fanatical sportsman. He had searchlights mounted on the roof (one is just visible near the flagpole), claiming that he liked to 'observe' the deer when they came down the mountainside at night to feed in his grounds! It is said that no less a person than a certain Mr Winston Spencer Churchill himself ordered the searchlights to be removed during the Great War. This photograph, taken *c.*1910, identifies the men at the boat simply as Stevens and W.

The road to the north-west runs beside Loch Rosque, rising at the watershed to 815 feet above sea-level, before making a long, gradual 1 in 12 descent through Glen Dochertie to Loch Maree. The glen is a supreme example of a glacial trough, formed when glaciers covered this land during the Ice Age about 3 million years ago. Many writers have claimed the unfolding panorama to be the finest in Scotland, and even Her Majesty was impressed, for she noted in her journal, '. . . from the top of the hill you go down a very grand pass called Glen Dochart. Here Loch Maree came in view most beautifully.' (Queen Victoria, 1877).

Postman John Mackenzie of Melvaig operated the Gairloch to Achnasheen mail service, and here is the three horse brake (known locally as 'the machine') in Glen Dochertie, *c.*1910. The driver's passenger is the formidable Miss Haig, one-time manageress of the Gairloch Hotel. (Photograph reproduced here by kind permission of Gairloch Heritage Museum).

The predominance of the horse in town and country ensured a steady supply of work for the blacksmith. He shod horses and mended agricultural implements, and at the Kinlochewe Smithy he was also the wheelwright, undertaking repairs to anything from the mail-coach to carriages, farm carts and wagons. Formerly an absolute mainstay of the local economy, the blacksmith's role diminished in importance with the increasing popularity of the motor-car and the introduction of the farm tractor during the Second World War.

The distinctive peaks, ridges and corries of Ben Eighe ('File Peak') and its outliers guard the glens north to Loch Maree and west to Torridon. The mountain overshadows the Kinlochewe Hotel which occupies a strategic position where routes converge, a factor which influenced the building of a posting house here over 300 years ago.

Glen Torridon, 'scented with thyme and bog-myrtle', carries the lonely road 11 miles to the head of Upper Loch Torridon, a remote area as easily reached by sea as by land until 1963 when the new road to Shieldaig was opened. Here one is among some of the oldest rocks known to man, perhaps 1,000 million years old – so ancient that no fossils have been found, indicating that the rock was laid down before life first appeared on earth. The rugged tiers, crags and buttresses of Ben Liathach ('the Grey One', 3,456 feet) draw the eye from every direction.

Annat, Upper Loch Torridon, *c.*1905. In the middle distance, Ben Damph mansion house lies among trees. Built in 1887 by the first Earl of Lovelace, it formed the hub of the 33,000 acre estate. After the death of the fourth Earl in December 1964 the property became the Loch Torridon Hotel, and sadly portraits of Lovelace ancestors no longer grace the walls of this former grand shooting lodge.

There was once a gun room here, fitted out with marble slab, scales for weighing fish and a book for recording the catch. Any remaining space was filled with a variety of rods, nets and boots. The notice displayed over the door 25 years ago would strike a chord with many fishermen: 'He riseth up early in the morning and disturbeth the whole household. He goeth forth full of hope. When the day is far spent he returneth, smelling of strong drink, and the truth is not in him.'

Torridon village, *c*.1907.

Fassaig (or Fasag), squeezed between the screes of Liathach and the shore, was created during the mid-19th century Clearances when crofters were evicted from their traditional lands to make way for sheep. The narrow, switchback road reveals breathtaking scenery along its 9 mile length. After negotiating the Bealach na Gaoithe ('Pass of the Wind') and Upper Diabaig, a final dramatic descent is made to the shore. Motorists beware!

Duncan Darroch died in 1910, but in 1872 he was the original proprietor of the Torridon Estate. In 1886 he sold 12,000 acres of the southern portion of his lands to William King-Noel, Earl of Lovelace, for £36,000; this became the nucleus of the Ben Damph Estate. This photograph of Torridon House encircled by Ben Alligin and Ben Dearg was adapted by the Darroch family as a Christmas greetings card, and posted at Torridon Post Office on 22 December 1905.

Branching sharply downhill from the 'main road', this track served Inveralligin on the northern shore of Upper Loch Torridon, *c*.1935. Crofting and fishing sustained this community, and up until the 1914-1918 War small boats were built here. This remote coast was far from the law, and in days past illegal distilling of whisky was rife, as elsewhere in the Highlands.

From Upper Diabaig a stony track twists and turns steeply downhill to Lower Diabaig and journey's end by the jetty, *c.*1935. The descent, either on foot or by car, will prove an unforgettable experience for most travellers.

The SS *Claymore*, supplying one of the remotest locations in mainland Britain, *c.*1914; her regular calls ensured the very survival of such tiny communities. Diabaig school can be seen (left). Before undertaking the steep, hair-raising climb from the shore for the return journey to Torridon village, motorists should offer up a prayer for safe deliverance!

On the mountain slopes of Ben Eighe (left) just beyond Kinlochewe, a 10,507 acre National Nature Reserve was established in 1951, the first of its kind in Britain. Of particular interest are the native Scots pines, a mere fragment of the formerly extensive Great Wood of Caledon, which covered much of northern Scotland 8,000 years ago.

Long regarded as a gem of classical Highland beauty, Loch Maree is over 12 miles in length and has a maximum depth of 360 feet. Some of the 27 wooded islets have religious and historical associations, while others are linked with romance or superstition. The stately mass of Slioch (3,217 feet) guards the southern end of the loch, while the western side carries the only road in this region (foreground), constructed just over 150 years ago.

Built in 1872, the small hotel at Talladale stood on a narrow, winding road beside Loch Maree, and on 12 September, 1877 the landlord, James Hornsby, ('a very nice quiet, youngish man'), awaited the arrival of a very important guest and her party who would be staying for the next six days. One suspects there was some tension in the air even though all arrangements had been put in hand some weeks previously, and the royal visitor now awaited had been preceded by her personal staff from Balmoral, and her own bed. After a change of horses at Kinlochewe and an 'enchanting' drive along the lochside, the carriages conveying Queen Victoria and the royal party arrived at the Loch Maree Hotel a little after 7 p.m. Her small bedroom on the first floor overlooked the loch, while from the adjoining sitting-room she could see Slioch. Her Majesty was delighted with the hotel. On the ensuing days she toured the district including Glen Torridon and Kerrysdale, visited the islands in the loch, and gave her name to some waterfalls at nearby Slattadale. At night, state papers demanded her attention, and the oil lamps burned well into the small hours. She eventually departed with great regret, hoping to return again, but she never did. The royal coat of arms is visible on the chimney-stack, near the entrance porch, *c.*1910.

The hotel was again in the news, only less happily so, in 1922. 'Seeing double' is often the cause of much mirth and ribald comment, and so it proved to be on 15 August when a guest failed to appear for breakfast citing double vision as the reason. However, mounting alarm spread as one guest after another remained in their rooms reporting symptoms which included dizziness, sickness, blurred vision and difficulty in speaking. Eventually paralysis developed making speech impossible, so that the sufferers who remained conscious throughout, but unable to speak, communicated only in writing. Despite frantic efforts by several medical practitioners, the nearest of whom resided 10 miles away, (and the hotel had no telephone at this time), six guests and two ghillies died over the next few days. Overwhelming forensic evidence later proved that preserved, potted wild duck served in sandwiches for the previous day's picnic lunches had been contaminated, and responsible for the tragedy. As *The Lancet*, the Journal of the British Medical Association, subsequently reported, the type of food poisoning was determined as bacillus botulinus (botulism), the first outbreak of its kind known to have occurred in Britain.

Sir Kenneth Mackenzie of Gairloch commissioned the carving of this memorial stone which is mounted on the line of the former road, immediately opposite the hotel. It reads 'On the 12th day of September, 1877, Queen Victoria came to see Loch Maree and the surrounding district. She remained six nights at the inn opposite, and in her gracious condescension willed that this stone should be a remembrance of the pleasure she found in coming to this part of Ross-shire'.

ONE DAY'S SEA-TROUT FISHING ON LOCH MAREE, ONE ROD.
30 TROUT, WEIGHING 31 POUNDS.

Loch Maree is famous for salmon, and more especially for sea-trout. It is uncertain whether this haul in the early years of the present century constituted a record of any kind, but plainly one fisherman would have been delighted with his day's sport.

At Letterewe, on the roadless eastern shore of Loch Maree, Sir George Hay of Megginch (later High Chancellor of Scotland) commenced iron working, 'casting great guns' in 1607, thereby giving birth to the Scottish iron industry. Each furnace devoured 120 acres of woodland annually, causing the felling of much of the surrounding forest. Letterewe House (seen here *c.*1910), at one time a seat of the Mackenzies, lay on an ancient trackway to the west used before 1845 by travellers and the post runner from Dingwall. His arduous route brought him through Strath Bran, Glen Dochertie via Letterewe to Flowerdale and Poolewe. For him the sight of this remote house in the woods must have been heaven-sent!

The inn and jetty, Badachro, *c.*1910. Situated on the south side of Loch Gairloch, Badachro was formerly an important fishing station. Cod, herring and ling were traded and cured here, as well as on two neighbouring islands, Dry Island and Isle Horrisdale.

Badachro, *c.*1910. For centuries Loch Gairloch was renowned for its cod fishery, the most constant and regularly productive of any on the coasts of Scotland. In 1884, some 80,000 cod, as well as significant numbers of other fish, passed though local processing stations, either cured or fresh. Salted, pickled or dried, they found ready markets in Ireland and Spain. The cod is all but fished out, and nowadays the catch consists mainly of shellfish, prepared and frozen at large modern industrial units at nearby Gairloch pier, much of it still bound for Spain.

Glen Cottage, Charleston, *c.*1895. The former factor's house of the Gairloch Estate stands amid luxuriant gardens and well-tilled land. Tall trees now surround the entrance gate to the cottage, renamed Glen Lodge, and the steading (left) has made way for Woodside, a bungalow reached by a separate driveway from the road.

These lands, which were in the possession of the Mackenzies of Gairloch and Conon for 500 years, formed the heart of the Gairloch Estate, once 170,000 acres in extent, although much reduced today. Locals knew the glen as Am Baile Mòr, and the house just visible among the trees in the centre of the photograph, as An Tigh Dige ('The Moat House'). In Victorian times, tourists from the south called the glen Flowerdale on account of the profusion of wild flowers, and this name has endured for both glen and house. In this photograph, *c.*1910, a narrow road to the bridge squeezes between the white building (formerly the post office, but now Inchgowan, a private residence), and the Old Inn built in the 1790s, originally a change-house for horses and coaches. Mrs Mackenzie administered the post office for some 60 years, her services being recognised by the presentation of a Coronation Medal in 1953.

Just to the left of the bridge (previous photograph), a carriage-drive to Flowerdale House leads up the glen, passing an old ice-house on the way. An Tigh Dige, built in 1738, took its name from an even earlier dwelling, and was the first slated house in the locality.

Following the 1904 extension which doubled its size, Flowerdale became M-gabled and two rooms deep. Contrary to popular belief, Cabinet meetings have not always been held in London. During the Great War, David Lloyd George and his Cabinet found it necessary to meet here on more than one occasion. The Prime Minister was allocated a spacious flat, while Mr Winston Churchill, then a Junior Secretary, had to make do with a tiny attic room.

The SS *Claymore*, seen here at Gairloch Pier, was a beautifully proportioned ship of 720 tons which served the Scottish west coast all year round between 1881 and 1931, carrying cargo, passengers and livestock.

Clean, golden sands and safe beaches drew holiday-makers in Victorian and Edwardian times, just as they do today. An Dun, the promontory (centre), is the site of an Iron Age fort.

Gairloch Hotel, 1893. The west facing rooms of this magnificently situated hotel look across to Skye and the Outer Hebrides. Built in 1872, a large posting establishment was maintained. Coaches toured the district, met MacBrayne steamers at the pier and, close by, Mr MacIver stabled his horses operating the Achnasheen mail service. The tall pair of steps to the right of the coach assisted mounting and dismounting. For some years this 150 bed hotel and the one at Talladale were both in the ownership of James Hornsby who had entertained Queen Victoria at Loch Maree in 1877. (See also page 96).

The hotel was a stage on the Scottish Automobile Club's reliability tests of 1909.

Miss Catherine Mackenzie's relatives were tenant farmers and stone-masons from Slattadale. About 1912 they commenced building this house at Achtercairn bringing quarried stone to the site by horse and cart, but the upheaval caused by the Great War resulted in the building never being completed as originally intended. Tor-na-Hulidhe operated as a guest-house between the wars, but the introduction of food rationing in 1939 brought this to an end; thereafter rooms were let. Miss Mackenzie was an early subscriber to the telephone, having the number Gairloch 9. She died in the 1970s at the age of 97.

A scattering of houses, well-tended crofts and a cluster of buildings near the shore – this view of Strath was taken by an unknown photographer about 85 years ago. Stand on the rising ground of the Poolewe road above Achtercairn and make a comparison today!

Strath, *c*.1915. For two centuries the village has been the commercial centre of the Gairloch area. Note the smithy (right) and, just beyond, the post office.

Roderick Maclean, blacksmith and wheelwright at work about the time of World War II. His services were much in demand, for in this rural economy horses still worked the land.

Unsurprisingly, the miller, too, was a person of local significance, and another mainstay of the community. The earliest meal mill in Strath was built in 1619; this is the later 18th century water-driven mill, sited in the centre of the village on the seaward side of The Square. Corn was brought here from a wide area to be ground by the Forbes family from 1870. When operations ceased in 1922, Roderick Forbes was the last of a long line of millers. Demolished in the 1930s, no trace now remains of this once important building.

Strath, *c*.1915. Curious residents watch the photographer at work. The house (right) started life as the cottage hospital and was later a girls' school, while the building in the background is now the Millcroft Hotel, a name which perpetuates memories of the vanished mill.

Carn Dearg, two miles west of Strath, is a distinctive Victorian house built by George Corson which was later gifted to the SYHA by the late Sir Frederick Wolff Ogilvie and his wife. It is said that the unusually high chimney-stacks act as a navigational aid for mariners. Since 13 May 1932, excellent facilities have been provided for those tramping the north-western Highlands. Old time hostellers recall with affection lighting the lamps at twilight and drawing water from a well across the road.

The Gairloch Hotel arranged combined coach and boat excursions on Loch Maree. Originally, tourists were driven to Croftbraefoot (half a mile from Poolewe), descending by a narrow lane to a landing-place on the River Ewe where boats awaited. The 8 mile row to Talladale (Loch Maree Hotel) was spectacular. Later, between 1883 and 1911, the steamer SS *Mabel*, a 45 foot vessel of 30 tons, operated a more sophisticated service from a small landing-stage near Tollie Farm. This served Talladale, Letterewe (Furnace) and the head of Loch Maree where a coach connection could be made to Achnasheen.

Poolewe village, 1902. 'The village consists chiefly of a long row of houses, terminated seawards by a very comfortable little inn. The Glasgow steamer calls once a fortnight'. (M. J. B. Baddeley's *Thorough Guide*, 1884).

The hotel in the 1930s.

Pool House, 1902. Born in 1842, the third son of Sir Francis Mackenzie, 5th baronet and 12th laird of Gairloch, Osgood Hanbury Mackenzie lived for part of his life in this house. Author of the classic book *A Hundred Years in the Highlands,* he created the now internationally famous sub-tropical gardens at nearby Inverewe.

The River Ewe, the shortest of rivers, being just two miles in length, tumbles under this fine keyed stone arch bridge near Pool House to enter Loch Ewe. There has been a bridge here for over 150 years. Before the spanning of Highland rivers, travellers faced disrupted journeys, and crofters experienced difficulties in moving stock – especially when the waters were in full spate.

The Inverness Society for the Education of the Poor in the Highlands established the first school in Inverasdale about 1819. The larger building to the right of the post office (centre) was the original school and church meeting-house, with the teacher or missionary living upstairs. The present 16-pupil school was recently in the news, being under threat of closure, but a reprieve has been granted . . . for the time being.

In 1862, at the age of 20, Osgood Mackenzie was gifted the adjoining estates of Kernsary and Inverewe. Two years later he commenced building a house and creating a garden on the barren, rocky promontory of Am Ploc Ard ('The High Lump') which then supported only stunted heather and crowberry. Soil and peat were imported in creels, thick shelter belts planted, and gradually fruits, exotic trees, shrubs and plants were introduced from all over the world to create a unique garden whose climate benefits from the warm waters of the Gulf Stream passing northwards up the coast. Mackenzie was still engaged on this mammoth undertaking at the time of his death in 1922, when his life's work was continued by his daughter who subsequently presented the gardens to The National Trust for Scotland in 1952. This oasis of colour and fertility is of interest in all seasons, attracting thousands of visitors from every part of the world. These pictures, dating from *c.*1905, show the gardens on the headland, a 'puffer' in the bay and Inverewe House, which was destroyed by fire in 1914.

Tinker's encampment, Loch Ewe, 1913.

The Hotel, Aultbea, *c*.1905. At this time Aultbea could be said to be only a clachan – a hamlet with scattered crofts, a school, a church and an hotel; the old saying was 'Education, Salvation and Damnation!'. During the Great War, the Grand Fleet once massed in Loch Ewe, and the Second World War saw much development when the loch became an important naval base and an assembly area for the Arctic convoys to Russia. In 1939, HMS *Nelson*, flagship of Invergordon mutiny fame (see *Easter Ross and the Black Isle*), was crippled by a magnetic mine laid by a German U-boat at the entrance to Loch Ewe.

In the latter half of the 19th century, the carriage road between Sand (3 miles north of Aultbea) and Dundonnell remained closed for more than 30 years, having degenerated through lack of maintenance into a rough bridle path. At Sand northbound travellers had a choice: a boat and four rowers could be hired at a cost of 23/- to convey them either to Dundonnell or Ullapool in 3 or 5 hours depending on wind and tide; alternatively they faced a 17 mile walk! A guidebook of the period details the sights to be experienced around Loch Gruinard, 'The dwellings are hovels – piles of loose stones with little or no cement – covered where the roof has not fallen in with thatch so long neglected as to resemble more than anything, an abandoned garden . . . holes for chimneys – and the light admitted by openings that seem to hint at a local ignorance of the repeal of the window-tax. Outside, the same utter lack of thrift and tidiness: what cultivation there is consists of grass and scanty oats'. This is Cabeg Hill, a long, steep and narrow 1 in 3 descent above Gruinard Bay, *c.*1945. At one time motorists dreaded a chance encounter on this notorious brae where a stretch of awkward reversing might be necessary to edge into a passing place.

Gruinard House, *c.*1910. The estate house and shooting lodge stands virtually on the shore overlooking the bay and island of the same name. Gruinard Island has a special place in the history of World War II as it was here in 1941 amid great secrecy that a team of Porton Down scientists began a series of top-secret germ warfare experiments using bacillus anthracis (anthrax) on sheep. The effects were so terrifying that details were to remain classified for decades; the resulting long-lasting contamination put the island out of bounds. By 1990 it had been officially decontaminated using a solution of formaldehyde and sea-water, and four years later the first lambs for over 50 years were safely born on 'Anthrax Island'.

The highway skirting Sail Mhor (2,508 feet) gradually becomes Destitution Road near Dundonnell. In the 1840s the potato crop failed in successive years owing to blight, causing widespread deprivation and famine in the Western Highlands and Islands. The landed proprietors, aided by Government grants, made substantial sums available for the building of new roads and the improvement of others, to provide work and food for the destitute. They became known as 'destitution roads', of which there are a number in Wester Ross. This one by Little Loch Broom was first tarmacadamed a century later in 1947.

Victorian travellers making for Dundonnell would pass scattered crofts with the whiff of peat reek at every door; fields of corn and hay fringing the loch coloured the landscape green and yellow. At Dundonnell they would find an inn 'affording excellent sleeping accommodation and, notwithstanding its remoteness, good fare'. Much changed and enlarged since this photograph *c.*1905, the hotel now also provides several essential local services – post and newspapers, school meals, petrol station and mountain rescue centre.

Dundonnell Lodge, 1893. From Dundonnell, a 7 mile hill-track to Altnaharrie crossed Strath Beag at the head of Little Loch Broom, passed around the lodge and climbed 800 feet to the col. A very precipitous, rough descent was made to the Altnaharrie Inn where a ferry connected with Ullapool, a mile distant, across Loch Broom. Horse and rowing-boat were the means of conveying the post and all manner of goods over this ancient drovers' route.

The small drovers' inn at Altnaharrie dates back at least 250 years. The 1884 edition of Mr Baddeley's *Thorough Guide* refers to 'the poor little public-house at Altnaharrie where the tourist will ferry across to Ullapool with all speed', but by 1915 it was 'a small hotel, well recommended'. It certainly still is today, as travellers come from near and far to experience the unique location and sample the internationally acclaimed cuisine. This picture shows vehicles on a rally *c.*1923 when the hill-track was still passable.

An Teallach ('The Forge'), seen here from Destitution Road, is one of the greatest mountains north of the Great Glen, consisting of ten rock peaks, all over 3,000 feet high. The old Gaelic name may originate from the mists and vapours that so often eddy around these crowded summits, crags and pinnacles where snow lies on the northern cornices well into early summer. Both a paradise and a challenge for the mountaineer, the jagged, serrated ridge is rated second only to that of the Cuillin Hills of Skye.

Passing though Dundonnell Forest (which despite its name is largely a wilderness of moor and bog), Destitution Road eventually joins the Garve to Ullapool road (built 1792) at Braemore – at a point known locally as 'The Junction'. Sir John Fowler (1817-1898) built Braemore House, or 'Castle' as it was known, in 1867. He was a consulting railway engineer, associated with a host of prestigious projects at home and abroad, including the building of the Metropolitan line on London's Underground, and the Forth Bridge (opened 1890) which he co-designed with Benjamin Baker. Knighted in 1885, he was also a JP and Deputy-Lieutenant of Ross-shire and Inverness-shire. Fowler was greatly attached to, and lavished money on, his 42,000 acre Braemore Estate, where, taking advantage of the favourable micro-climate just as Osgood Mackenzie had done at Inverewe, he made 'the wilderness blossom as the rose'. Sadly, in the early 1960s, dry-rot and other major defects resulted in the demolition of Braemore House. Interesting features still remain in the grounds – subway tunnels built for the horse stables, and a bridge at Auchindrean believed to be a prototype of a span for the world-famous Forth Railway Bridge. In July 1920, the Conditions of Sale of the Braemore Estate, which included the deer-forests of Braemore, Fain and Inverbroom, showed this rare photograph of the front hall and central staircase – opulence from a vanished age.

Corrieshalloch Gorge, once part of the Braemore Estate and now in the care of The National Trust for Scotland, is a stupendous ravine a mile in length where the Falls of Measach plunge 150 feet. Sir John Fowler designed the suspension footbridge, which has been measured at 246 feet above the chasm bottom – not a sight for the faint-hearted!

Leckmelm, 1893. Mr A. G. Pirie, an Aberdeen paper manufacturer, achieved a degree of notoriety when he set about clearing crofters from his Leckmelm Estate. The pretext was that their sheep and cattle were trespassing on the hill and his enclosures. His solution was an ingenious one; his tenants might remain in their cottages only if they kept no livestock. Without livestock, of course, they had no livelihood. The threat to clear the Estate and take down cottages after Martinmas 1880 put the issue beyond doubt. Reminiscent of enforced evictions elsewhere, it was a variation on an old Highland theme.

The Royal Hotel lies on the southern fringe of Ullapool, 'capital of Lochbroom'. It was to this long-established and busy hostelry that travellers of old came by way of either Dundonnell and Altnaharrie across Loch Broom, or from Garve over desolate Dirrie More. The mails, too, were brought the 32 miles from Garve by Mr Mackenzie's Garve and Ullapool Mail Service (see pages 54 and 96). Pictured *c*.1910, the Royal suffered a disastrous fire in the 1960s and was rebuilt.

This is the 'classic' view of Ullapool (*c*.1900) – a small village with orderly streets on a triangular spit of land protruding into the sheltered waters of Loch Broom. Across the loch, Ben Goleach (2,082 feet) looms on the skyline; the inn at Altnaharrie just out of view (left). Eleven centuries ago, Norse invaders were familiar with these western sea-lanes and, during the Clearances of the 18th and 19th centuries, many emigrant ships left this coast carrying dispossessed Highlanders to an uncertain future overseas. One such ship was the *Hector*, a vessel of 200 tons, which transported 200 Highlanders from Loch Broom in July 1773. A desperately miserable voyage of 11 weeks brought them ultimately to Pictou in Nova Scotia where, despite appalling privations, they eventually prospered.

Ullapool, one of three west coast developments by the British Fisheries Society, was founded in 1788 to exploit the very considerable resources of the adjacent Minch fishing-grounds, especially herring and white fish. Fifteen hundred acres of land were acquired on Loch Broom, and over £10,000 expended on laying out the new village and on public works to provide a pier, storehouses and an inn. This superb early aerial photograph shows the grid pattern adopted by the planners, and sharp-eyed residents will be able to identify many buildings including the Captain's Cabin, Fowler Memorial Clock, Caledonian Hotel, post office, 'Parliamentary' church of 1829 (now the Ullapool Museum), police station, village hall and Customs House with its semi-circular roof (top left).

Shore Street at the bottom of Quay Street, *c*.1905.

Erected in 1899, the ornate cast-iron memorial clock, dedicated to Sir John Fowler of Braemore, originally had two faces looking up and down Quay Street. Other Fowler family plaques have since been added to adorn the base of the column. This picture shows the clock in its original location, in the middle of the Argyle/Quay Street intersection; it was removed the few yards to its present position nearby in the 1960s.

Pultney Street. There was no globe street lighting in 1925 – in fact, none at all!

Fish curing called for vast quantities of salt. Salt duties were imposed in the reign of William III, making it a valuable commodity to be kept under lock and key at the Customs House. The tax was abolished in 1823, but the Customs House is still extant, known today as the Drill Hall.

Loch Broom has been a notable year-round fishing ground since at least the 16th century. The important herring season lasted from October to March, but the ways of the migratory herring are complex, and not fully understood. Towards the close of the 18th century there were boom years of abundance and prosperity which were followed in more than equal measure by years of scarcity and despair. The best herring are generally reckoned to be those caught in West Hebridean waters, and in the season Ullapool was hard pressed to accommodate the gutters, packers and curers seeking work. Scenes such as these at the pier, when scores of boats worked out of Loch Broom, reflect the importance of the Scottish fisheries as a whole, which, at the end of the 19th century, engaged upwards of 7,000 boats with an aggregate of 230,000,000 square yards of netting.

Some of the fisher girls chose to work at one port for the season, while others travelled with the boats which followed the shoals, thereby providing employment throughout the year at stations as far apart as Kinsale, Wick and Great Yarmouth. Skilled girls could gut and grade 60 herring a minute, and in the event of a glut they might work a 16 hour day. These girls, photographed in Point Street (now West Shore Street) 90 years ago, are working a deep farlin full of 'the silver darlings'. When the fishing was good, cooperage also flourished. The barrels, only ever used once, were often made of high quality American oak (although other woods were also used) and held between 700 and 1,000 herring, packed in layers of salt. Exported to the Mediterranean and the West Indies, huge quantities also went to Germany and Russia up to the 1914-1918 War; the value of herring cured in Scotland then amounted to over £1m annually.

Departing Ullapool for the north engenders thoughts of leaving one of the remoter outposts of civilisation. The traveller is dwarfed by the grandeur and increasing isolation of the terrain. At Ardmair the gracefully curved and steeply shelving bay faces Isle Martin (out of picture). The 393 acre island has early religious associations. In 1775 it was developed as a fishing station, complete with salt-house; the few older dwellings on the bay itself are thought to be of contemporaneous date. The huge dignified mass of Ben More Coigach (2,438 feet) blocks the view northwards.

Once part of the Cromartie Estates, the 20,000 acre Drumrunie Forest was the late Victorian sportsman's paradise. In 1890 the lodge was described as 'new and spacious' with 'seven principal bedrooms and ample accommodation for a butler and other servants'. Nearby Langwell was the home farm. The lodge stood above an artificial loch about a mile south of the junction with the Achiltibuie road, and in its final phase was an hotel. Rhododendrons now encroach on the silent, overgrown driveway which winds quickly up to a plateau where the building once stood. Pictured here *c.*1905, the lodge burned to the ground some 50 years later, and the remaining stonework was later dismantled for use elsewhere.

From Drumrunie the route to Achiltibuie lies westwards, initially following this road, which was built in 1882 to provide an alternative approach to Lochinver in Sutherland by way of Enard Bay. Narrow and single track, it is a gem to travel, especially in early summer when the gorse is in bloom. This photograph of 1893 shows the 4 mile long crescent-shaped Loch Lurgainn, and An Stac (Stac Polly), a most distinctive mountain which presents a variety of interesting shapes when viewed from different angles. (See also page 2).

Badentarbet Bay lies 12 miles by sea from Ullapool, and twice that distance by the only road, so a journey here is never a matter of chance, nor undertaken lightly. The bay and the straggling settlement of Achiltibuie overlook the islands and skerries of the Summer Isles at the entrance to Loch Broom. In the late 18th century herring curing stations were established on Ristol and the largest island Tanera More, which has a safe horse-shoe anchorage. At one time a salmon-fishing station operated at Badentarbet. MacBrayne boats called here on their regular sailings between Ullapool and Lochinver, and up to the Second World War the 1,000 ton passenger and cargo coaster SS *Lochbroom* was a familiar sight in the bay which became the 'port' for the Coigach district.

Admittedly there is some artistic licence here, but this *c.*1905 picture captures the essential characteristics of this community by the side of Loch Broom, amid the Coigach mountains.

The name C. E. Ross was over the hotel door from the 1930s until 1956. A visitor after the Second World War was charmed by the proprietors and two pretty Gaelic speaking waitresses who hailed from Gairloch, but it was Mrs Murray, the cook, who really caught his attention. A natural and quite untrained singer 'she had the most wonderful singing voice and sang Gaelic songs better than anyone I have ever heard'. He did not record her abilities as a cook!

The area is a mecca for the fisherman. Excellent deep sea-angling is available on Loch Broom, while fly-fishing is popular on the many hill lochs. The seasons are: sea-trout and salmon from end of June to end of September; brown trout are best from May to end of September.

Four miles beyond Achiltibuie, the lochside road ends at the Culnacraig crofts. An adventurous coastal footpath continues towards Ardmair under the western shoulder of Ben More Coigach which falls steeply into Loch Broom. In Victorian times, the postman from Ullapool brought the mails this way, habitually undertaking this feat of daring in the line of duty. Isle Martin is in view to the left.

The many islands and islets of irregular shape and size which comprise the Summer Isles are the higher remnants of a landscape drowned by the sea, and for nearly 300 years they formed part of the Cromartie Estates. At various times several have sustained a population, although today's inhabitants are mainly sea-birds and seals, and livestock grazing the summer pastures. To the south there are superb vistas towards the Torridon Highlands and Skye, but the eye is drawn westwards where the sun sets in ultimate splendour beyond the Outer Hebrides. There, far below the western seas, lies Tir nan Og, a legendary Celtic paradise bathed in eternal light and totally without darkness, where the Young of Heart never grow old.

xiv

Scotland.

GAIRLOCH HOTEL,

ROSS-SHIRE, N.B.

"The comforts are undoubted; the management is excellent."
Vide "TIMES," Sept. 8th, 1879.

:o:

This fine Hotel contains, besides its numerous Public Rooms, Suites of Apartments and 150 Beds.

Tourists and Families may now rely upon most comfortable Bedroom accommodation, which may be secured by telegram in passing North.

The situation of Gairloch Hotel connects it by well-appointed Coaches, and an ample Posting Establishment, with the Loch Maree Hotel at Talladale, and with the Highland Railway at Achnasheen Station; also by Mr. David Mac Brayne's splendid Daily Steamer Service with Portree (Skye), Oban and Glasgow.

Sea-bathing, Boating, and Sea-fishing can be enjoyed in rare perfection, and Visitors have the right of Rod-fishing for Trout on an excellent Loch in the near vicinity.

There are various interesting Drives and Excursions, including the Circular Tour by Road and Loch, in one day, of the finest local scenery. A Steamer has been placed on Loch Maree for the purposes of this Tour, and also to visit the various places of interest between Tolly and Kinlochewe, the extreme points of the Loch, as occasion may require.

Orders for Coach-seats and Apartments carefully attended to.

JAMES HORNSBY,
PROPRIETOR.

xv

Scotland.

LOCH MAREE.

LOCH MAREE HOTEL,

TALLADALE, ROSS-SHIRE, N.B.

The accommodation and comforts of this fine Hotel, which is the only one on Loch Maree, render it a charming Summer resort for Sportsmen, Tourists and Families.

Visitors have the privilege of Fishing on Loch Maree, which is well known to abound in salmon and sea-trout, together with the native fish, which run to a large size.

Several boats with boatmen are provided for enabling Visitors to fish on the Loch, or for making excursions to the numerous adjacent islands.

A steamer has been placed on Loch Maree (see preceding page).

Orders for Apartments or Conveyances carefully attended to.

JAMES HORNSBY,
PROPRIETOR.

Advertisements from M. J. B. Baddeley's *Thorough Guide,* 1884.

W. D. MACKENZIE
PROPRIETOR OF THE GARVE & ULLAPOOL
MAIL SERVICE.

CONNECTED WITH GARVE HOTEL.

CARS FOR HIRE.
LOCH FISHING.
GOLF.
PETROL PUMP. OILS.

TELEPHONE: NO. 8 ULLAPOOL.
TELEGRAMS : "ROYAL, ULLAPOOL."

ROYAL HOTEL,

ULLAPOOL, ROSS-SHIRE.

Royal Hotel letter-heading advertising the Garve and Ullapool Mail Service.